BRI
WA
& AUXILLIARIES

**HMS Hurworth and
HMS Cattistock**

THE ROYAL NAVY

"It is a curious paradox we now face. The prospect of a nuclear exchange has been very substantially reduced. However, the end of the Cold War and the collapse of the Soviet Union has led to instability and fragmentation the like of which has not been seen since World War II."

Malcolm Rifkind,
Secretary of State for Defence, July 1992

As the world emerges from the Cold War era, defence planners in the United Kingdom are caught between the uncertainties of an unpredictable international security environment, a Treasury which is exerting an increasingly tight reign on defence expenditure, and a public which inevitably expects some sort of peace dividend. The dichotomy is readily apparent. On the one hand there is an expanding spectrum of possible contingencies/commitments to cope with; on the other, resources are clearly in decline.

A Political Outlook

For the Royal Navy, this dilemma is indeed a serious one. The heavy burden of national and NATO directed tasks remains – along with other unwritten commitments. Under the Government's "Options for Change" plans first outlined in 1990 and latterly "Britain's Defence for the Nineties" the job must now be accomplished with a 20 per cent reduction in destroyers and frigates and an even deeper cut in the number of fleet submarines. This, when many officers were already seriously concerned about the overstretch of men and material.

Indeed, since 1979 the Royal Navy has seen destroyer and frigate numbers reduced by 42 per cent and submarines by 57 per cent, even before the latest cuts take effect. [1]

Simple statistics undeniably disguise the improvements in capability and operational efficiency which have been implemented over the last decade. For instance, the latest Type 23 frigates represent a quantum leap over the Leanders they replace, both in enhanced operational capability and reduced through-life cost. And at a unit price of around £130 million they offer real savings to the exchequer when compared to their Type 22 predecessors.

However, one ship can only be in one place at one time. If commitments remain constant, but hull numbers decline, then the burden on each individual ship becomes so much the greater. The consequence is an ever increasing strain on ships and their crews.

Force size is of course only one side of the equation. The proliferation of sophisticated weapons to potentially unstable or unfriendly regimes presents another challenge. Sea skimming anti-ship missiles, ultra-quiet conventional submarines, and modern long range strike aircraft have all found their way into the inventories of nations whose aspirations are at odds with those of the West. The availability of relatively cheap but modern

3

weapons from cash-starved Russia is of particular concern (Iran's acquisition of up to three "Kilo" class submarines is a case in point). It is thus incumbent on the Government to outline the threat it considers exists (or could exist) to the UK and its treaty partners, and thereby allow the Navy to purchase equipment to meet those threats from within its allocated resources.

There is no easy answer to the problem of quantity versus quality. A fine balance must be struck between the overall size of the fleet and the operational capability of individual units. The RN has opted to emphasise the latter – the nature of modern naval warfare is such that a relatively small design economy could result in the loss of a ship – but now treads a fine line as it attempts to avoid a dangerous disequilibrium.

If fleet overstretch is a worry, then equally disconcerting are question marks over the ability of Britain's merchant fleet to provide military sealift support in time of war or crisis. Although the Ministry of Defence proclaims its satisfaction with the availability of chartered shipping, independent analysis suggests that there are no longer enough militarily useful merchant ships on the British register to fulfil the national sealift requirement. [2] The basis on which the UK Government would expect foreign crews to enter a potential war zone in support of British interests is hardly clear.

Such a situation is perhaps to be expected from a Government which appears quite content to see market forces override national security interests. But it is also rooted in a more fundamental decline.

As an island nation, until recently with an empire to oversee, the UK has traditionally attached great importance to the maintenance and projection of sea power. However, over the last two decades continental Europe has increasingly become the focus for Britain's economic policies and security interests. This has had serious implications for Britain's maritime fleets, both merchant and naval.

In truth, the independent projection of sea power across vast oceans is something which Britain would neither desire, nor, it would seem, can it afford, in the nineties . . . Another Falklands-style campaign would test present capabilities to the absolute limit, but resource constraints place very serious doubts as to whether the navy could provide for all reasonable contingencies.

For this reason, collective defence will undoubtedly assume ever greater importance. Multinational forces, under the auspices of organisations such as NATO, the Western European Union and the United Nations, will bear a greater weight on their shoulders in all areas of naval activity, as operations in the Gulf and off Yugoslavia have recently demonstrated. The question must surely be asked however, if all the governments of a multi-national force would approve the use of their navies in what could be seen as a solely "British problem".

The creation of an Anglo-French Standing Naval Force would provide a basis to assess just how far the theory of bilateral operations could be pursued in practice. A multitude of potential problems – command structures, operating procedures, logistical support, and, of course, language – would have to be addressed. But if pan-European defence cooperation is to amount to more than simple rhetoric it is surely a concept worth pursuing. One can almost hear the "mutterings" from within the RN as this is being written!

A Fleet for the 90s

Under the plans laid out under "Options for Change", the future strength of the RN is envisaged at:

* 3 small aircraft carriers (CVSGs)
* 2 amphibious assault ships (LPDs)
* 1 amphibious helicopter carrier (LPH)
* about 40 destroyers and frigates (DDGs/FFGs)
* 34 mine countermeasures vessels (MCMVs)
* 4 nuclear ballistic missile submarines (SSBNs)
* 12 nuclear attack submarines (SSNs)
* 4 diesel-electric submarines (SSKs)

As can be seen in the following pages cuts in ship and submarine numbers have already accounted for most of the remaining Leander class frigates and Oberon SSKs. The few remaining units in both classes are now due to be withdrawn by the end of 1993. Next to go will be the six Type 21 frigates. At the same time more of the new Type 23 frigates will be entering service, but falling construction rates will lead to a substantial reduction in the total number of hulls. There is also a question mark over the continued operation of the four Type 22 Batch 1 frigates, which lack both a towed array sonar and a modern command system. Indeed, although senior RN officers believe they will be able to maintain about 38 escorts in commission, there are well-founded fears that the size of the RN's destroyer/frigate force could slip towards just 30 ships by the early years of the next century.

Under plans announced in early 1992, the RN is to finally get new and much-needed amphibious shipping in the shape of two assault ships plus a helicopter carrier. A "real order" has yet however to be placed. Given the increased emphasis on flexible, mobile rapid reaction forces, this £500 million renewal programme represents excellent value for money when compared to, say, the European Fighter Aircraft. It is sad to note then that senior civil servants are known to have pressed for the scrapping of the RN's amphibious forces even after a Ministerial commitment to their retention.

Numerically, the Future Frigate – intended as a replacement for the current Type 42 air defence destroyers – will be the RN's most important surface shipbuilding programme in the long term. Up to 12 new ships are required, with the first vessel planned to enter service in 2002. Now being studied as a joint Anglo-French project, there are also signs that Italy too may wish to collaborate. Care must be taken to avoid a repetition of the earlier NFR-90 fiasco, when eight NATO navies attempted to design a standard frigate despite disparate timescales and differing requirements. Failure was inevitable.

According to the RN, the capabilities of the Future Frigate will represent a "step change" from the ships they replace. As well as deploying a Support Defence Missile System (SDMS) and a new Very Short Range Air Defence system (VSRAD), the Type 42 replacement will also have a sophisticated Combat Management System likely to include a number of automated decision aids.

The service has also made clear that the Future Frigate will need to offer more than just air defence for the fleet. With fewer hulls in the water, each platform must offer greater flexibility to undertake a variety of roles. Consequently, the new escort will offer significant anti-surface and anti-submarine capabilities.

A new medium calibre gun, perhaps a 155mm weapon, will be fitted for naval gunfire support and anti-surface roles, while a new long range surface-to-surface guided weapon, intended to replace the current Exocet and Harpoon anti-ship missiles, is also planned.

The Future Frigate will also have a hull-mounted medium range sonar (with mine avoidance capability), a torpedo defence system, and an embarked EH.101 Merlin helicopter. Merlin, now planned to enter RN service in 1998, will set new standards in airborne anti-submarine warfare (ASW).

The order for 44 Merlins placed with prime contractors Westland/IBM-ASIC in 1991 signalled that the RN intends to remain a major force in ASW and the wider undersea warfare arena. Indeed, the RN's undersea equipment modernisation programme is likely to remain a significant part of the UK defence budget, the demise of the Soviet submarine threat leading to a change in the ASW situation which senior officers describe as more one of emphasis than of substance. Whilst old superpower tensions may have gone, Russian submarine capability remains significant and is improving in qualitative terms. Elsewhere, the proliferation of quiet, modern conventional submarines also continues as Third World navies add to their fleets. This also means that ASW operations are now more likely to occur outside of the traditional NATO sphere, possibly in shallow waters where sonar propagation is poor and oceanographic data is limited.

Three major programmes – the Spearfish torpedo, the Batch 2 Trafalgar class nuclear attack submarine (SSN), and the tactical weapons system update for the Swiftsure and Trafalgar class SSNs – are crucial to the maintenance of the RN's world class ASW capability.

Spearfish, regarded as the most advanced heavyweight torpedo in the world, has been under development by Marconi Underwater Systems Limited since the early 1980s, with total development costs estimated at £900 million. But so far the company has produced just 100 torpedoes under the initial development contract. At £9 million per torpedo questions are rightly being asked . . . A main production order is expected at the end of 1993.

Following the cancellation of the SSN20 submarine programme last year, studies are now proceeding for an improved Trafalgar class SSN which is planned to enter service early in the next century. In the meantime, it is planned to modernise the 12 existing Swiftsure and Trafalgar class SSNs with new sonar, data handling and command equipment.

Mine countermeasures is a source of both pride and frustration for the RN. The performance of the "Hunt" class ships in the Gulf won widespread acclaim from allied navies, yet the Ministry of Defence has since seen fit to postpone further orders for the new Sandown class minehunter. It is now suggested that tenders will be invited for further Sandowns in 1993 but even then it appears likely that the requirement will be for no more than five ships, limiting the class to just ten hulls. Up to 20 were originally envisaged before the Treasury took over the running of the Royal Navy.

On a brighter note, plans are now underway for the 13 "Hunt" class MCMVs to undergo a mid-life update which will introduce improvements to the ships' command system and enhanced sonar performance against ground mines.

It is also known that studies are already in hand to identify replacements for the current Invincible class support carriers (CVSGs) in parallel with moves to examine options for a

Sea Harrier Replacement (SHR) and a future airborne early warning (AEW) aircraft. All three requirements are seen as key elements of a single operational package to maintain long range air defence for the fleet in the post-2010 period.

Pre-feasibility studies for a SHR are already underway and Defence Staff sources say that a Staff Target will be issued in 1993. The RN has already held discussions with the US Navy to establish common ground on future development as it is understood that the SHR requirement will closely match that of the US Marine Corps STOVL Strike Fighter (SSF).

It has been confirmed that fleet AEW will remain in the hands of the Sea King AEW.2A until about 2010. In the meantime all ten aircraft will be modernised under a recently announced Mission Systems Update programme. Preliminary concept evaluation studies looking at options for a CVSG replacement (CVSG(R)) have already been completed. These are understood to have found in favour of building new carriers in the order of 20,000 - 25,000 tonnes standard displacement.

However, senior RN officials acknowledge that tough battles will have to be fought with Ministers and the Treasury to get the go ahead for a new fleet of carriers and embarked air groups. The decision will be central to the ability of the Navy to fight in waters out of the range of land based air cover.

Hopefully the lesson of both Falklands and Gulf campaign will be repeated over and over again as inter-service squabbles are aired within the Treasury and MoD.

A Value for Money Navy?

As the size of the Navy vote declines in real terms, it is essential that the RN gets the best return on its expenditure. There is no denying that strenuous efforts have been made to achieve greater efficiency across the board in recent years. Greater personal accountability and new financial management practices are to be welcomed.

The RN is also finding itself in an increasingly "competitive" market. In mid-1992 it became known that the Ministry of Agriculture, Fisheries and Food was considering the use of a commercial contractor to perform UK offshore patrols, currently undertaken by the Fishery Protection Squadron (FPS), on the grounds that "privatisation" would save money.

The proposal remains under scrutiny. But naval sources point out that the FPS also plays a vital role in anti-terrorist surveillance and pollution control, as well as providing support for HM Customs in the interception of illegal immigrants, drug runners and other miscreants. How can the Government apply a market value to these functions?

As a nation where 84 companies a day are calling in the receivers/liquidators (at the time of writing) even school children are asking what sort of country they will be living in a few years time. When they point out, we, as a nation, are very good at spending money for defence, health care, social services but rapidly losing our once major industrial base to pay for all these necessities of life ı˙ is time the older generation did some listening. One has serious doubts that the "spenders" in MoD have realised what a predicament the nation is in and that so many top rate industrialists are joining the dole queue. If, as a nation, we are unable to "make things to make money" how can the nation afford to defend itself properly without incurring massive overseas debts? Service and civilian staff within the MoD empire still consider they are all vital to the defence of the realm whereas any real commercial organisation would have given then a gold watch and a P45 years ago.

With whole industries being decimated at the stroke of a pen (remember the coal industry?) just wait for the public outcry when the unions start acting for public sector pay rises. Redundancy programmes are all very well if those being made redundant have a future for the well being of UK plc but with many good people heading, like it or not, for the dole queue one wonders why one has not heard of a scheme "in the national interest" for all staff to take a reasonable pay reduction on the principle of "better a job than none at all" – a very common occurrence in industry these days. We have overpaid ourselves too long . . . Even after "the cuts" there are still parts of the naval scene where one comes across people doing "non jobs" in the so called "lean" navy of the 90s. Too many phones still ring unanswered on a Friday afternoon which must tell a story.

More Cuts . . .

At the time of writing it was only a matter of time before an announcement was made regarding the future of the Naval Base at Portland, the joint service/civilian Fleet Maintenance and Repair organisation at Portsmouth and the entire future of the Royal Naval Reserve. No one was expecting good news as the Royal Navy is shrunk in size by the Treasury. Cuts in shore support and refit capacity should be expected – even demanded.

A small fleet only needs a small back up team. The RN is not in business simply to provide work in areas of high unemployment – if it can, that is simply a bonus.

Public Relations

The biggest surprise during 1992 has been how the image of all of our defence forces have dramatically dropped in the eyes of the majority of the public. Just ten years ago they were all, in the view of the public, national heros after events in the South Atlantic. Now, in what really is a far more unstable world, members of the forces are about as unpopular as the VAT inspector or Poll Tax investigator. Memories are very short.

It is a sad reflection on society that, since the Berlin Wall came down many of our forces are seen as a simple "drain on national resources", overpaid, with excellent perks, with some "stress free" jobs in the four corners of the world. This really does seem to be how the public relates to an organisation it rarely sees "firsthand". The RN Presentation team potters around the country preaching to a, basically converted, hand picked audience and no doubt thinks it has "cracked the problem" of PR. There is a much greater problem to confront than, I hereby submit, is realised.

Jobs in the dockyard and shipbuilding ports are "essential" for the local workforce but you try and persuade the general public in Leeds of Cardiff they should pay for them... the cry is "we all live in a much safer world these days".

I have my doubts...

1. Capt Richard Sharpe, Jane's Fighting Ships 1992-3
2. Eric Grove, The State of British Merchant Shipping – The Defence Dimension. UK Chamber of Shipping Report, July 1992.

SHIPS OF THE ROYAL NAVY
Pennant Numbers

Ship	Pennant Number	Ship	Pennant Number
Aircraft Carriers		BEAVER	F93
		BRAVE	F94
INVINCIBLE	R05	LONDON	F95
ILLUSTRIOUS ●	R06	SHEFFIELD	F96
ARK ROYAL	R07	COVENTRY	F98
		CORNWALL	F99
Destroyers		AMAZON	F169
		ACTIVE	F171
BRISTOL ●	D23	AMBUSCADE	F172
BIRMINGHAM	D86	ARROW	F173
NEWCASTLE	D87	ALACRITY	F174
GLASGOW	D88	AVENGER	F185
EXETER	D89	LANCASTER	F229
SOUTHAMPTON	D90	NORFOLK	F230
NOTTINGHAM	D91	ARGYLL	F231
LIVERPOOL	D92	MARLBOROUGH	F233
MANCHESTER	D95	IRON DUKE	F234
GLOUCESTER	D96	MONMOUTH	F235
EDINBURGH	D97	MONTROSE	F236
YORK	D98	WESTMINSTER	F237
CARDIFF	D108	NORTHUMBERLAND	F238
		RICHMOND	F239
Frigates		**Submarines**	
SIRIUS	F40		
ARGONAUT	F56	ORACLE	S16
ANDROMEDA	F57	OPOSSUM	S19
SCYLLA	F71	OPPORTUNE	S20
CUMBERLAND	F85	RESOLUTION	S22
CAMPBELTOWN	F86	REPULSE	S23
CHATHAM	F87	RENOWN	S26
BROADSWORD	F88	UPHOLDER	S40
BATTLEAXE	F89	UNSEEN	S41
BRILLIANT	F90	URSULA	S42
BRAZEN	F91	UNICORN	S43
BOXER	F92		

Ship	Pennant Number	Ship	Pennant Number
TRENCHANT	S91	NURTON	M1166
TALENT	S92	SHERATON	M1181
TRIUMPH	S93	SANDOWN	M101
VALIANT	S102	INVERNESS	M102
SCEPTRE	S104	CROMER	M103
SPARTAN	S105	WALNEY	M104
SPLENDID	S106	BRIDPORT	M105
TRAFALGAR	S107	WAVENEY	M2003
SOVEREIGN	S108	CARRON	M2004
SUPERB	S109	DOVEY	M2005
TURBULENT	S110	HELFORD	M2006
TIRELESS	S117	HUMBER	M2007
TORBAY	S118	BLACKWATER	M2008
		ITCHEN	M2009

Assault Ships

Ship	Pennant Number	Ship	Pennant Number
		HELMSDALE ●	M2010
		ORWELL	M2011
FEARLESS	L10	RIBBLE ●	M2012
INTREPID ●	L11	SPEY	M2013
		ARUN	M2014

Minesweepers & Minehunters

Patrol Craft

Ship	Pennant Number	Ship	Pennant Number
BRECON	M29	PEACOCK	P239
LEDBURY	M30	PLOVER	P240
CATTISTOCK	M31	STARLING	P241
COTTESMORE	M32	LEEDS CASTLE	P258
BROCKLESBURY	M33	REDPOLE	P259
MIDDLETON	M34	KINGFISHER	P260
DULVERTON	M35	CYGNET	P261
BICESTER	M36	ARCHER	P264
CHIDDINGFOLD	M37	DUMBARTON CASTLE	P265
ATHERSTONE	M38	BITER	P270
HURWORTH	M39	SMITER	P272
BERKELEY	M40	PURSUER	P273
QUORN	M41	ANGLESEY	P277
BRINTON	M1114	ALDERNEY	P278
WILTON	M1116	BLAZER	P279
IVESTON ●	M1151	DASHER	P280
KELLINGTON ●	M1154		

Ship	Pennant Number	Ship	Pennant Number
PUNCHER	P291	MESSINA	A107
CHARGER	P292	ROEBUCK	A130
RANGER	P293	HECLA	A133
TRUMPETER	P294	HERALD	A138
JERSEY	P295	ENDURANCE	A171
GUERNSEY	P297	IRONBRIDGE	A311
SHETLAND	P298	BULLDOG	A317
ORKNEY	P299	IXWORTH	A318
LINDISFARNE	P300	BEAGLE	A319
		DATCHET	A357
Survey Ships & RN		CHALLENGER ●	K07
Manned Auxiliaries			
BRITANNIA	A00	● Ships in reserve/long refit	
GLEANER	A86		

This book is updated and re-issued every December. Keep up to date … Don't miss the new edition.

Phone 0579 343663 for details.

HMS Vanguard

VANGUARD CLASS

Ship	Pennant Number	Completion Date	Builder
VANGUARD		1992	Vickers
VICTORIOUS			Vickers
VIGILANT			Vickers

Displacement 15,000 tons (dived) **Dimensions** 150m x 13m x 12m **Speed** 25 + dived **Armament** 16 x Lockheed Trident 2 (D5) missiles, 4 Torpedo Tubes **Complement** 135 (Two crews).

Notes

VANGUARD sailed from her builders at Barrow in October 1992 for initial sea trials. A fourth vessel has been ordered.

● LA PHOT BALL

HMS Renown

RESOLUTION CLASS

Ship	Pennant Number	Completion Date	Builder
RESOLUTION	S22	1967	Vickers
REPULSE	S23	1968	Vickers
RENOWN	S26	1968	C. Laird

Displacement 8,400 tons (submerged) **Dimensions** 130m x 10m x 9m **Speed** 25 knots **Armament** 16 Polaris missiles, 6 Torpedo Tubes **Complement** 147 (Two crews).

Notes
These three nuclear-powered Polaris submarines have been the United Kingdom's contribution to NATO's strategic nuclear deterrent since the late 1960's. Despite the age of these vessels and, well publicised technical problems, one of these submarines is constantly on patrol. Thanks to their high speed, long endurance underwater, and advanced sonar and electronic equipment they have little fear of detection.
Each submarine carries 16 Polaris two-stage ballistic missiles, powered by solid fuel rocket motors, 9.45 metres long, 1.37 metres diameter and weighting 12,700 kilogrammes with a range of 2,500 miles. REVENGE paid off 1992. The 3 remaining vessels of the Class will gradually leave the Fleet as the Vanguard Class come into service.

● HMS NEPTUNE

HMS Valiant

VALIANT CLASS

Ship	Pennant Number	Completion Date	Builder
VALIANT	S102	1966	Vickers

Displacement 4,900 tons (dived) **Dimensions** 87m x 10m x 8m **Speed** 28 knots + **Armament** 6 Torpedo Tubes **Complement** 103.

Notes

The "last of the first" truly British nuclear powered submarines in service. CHURCHILL and DREADNOUGHT – the forerunners of this class are awaiting disposal (by scrap or sinking) at Rosyth. CONQUEROR, COURAGEOUS and WARSPITE at Devonport. VALIANT spent most of 1992 under refit/repair and has only a limited life in the active Fleet. Discussions continue regarding the safe disposal of these vessels but no solution seems imminent.

● HMS NEPTUNE

HMS Sceptre

SWIFTSURE CLASS

Ship	Pennant Number	Completion Date	Builder
SCEPTRE	S104	1978	Vickers
SPARTAN	S105	1979	Vickers
SPLENDID	S106	1980	Vickers
SOVEREIGN	S108	1974	Vickers
SUPERB	S109	1976	Vickers

Displacement 4,500 tons dived **Dimensions** 83m x 10m x 8m **Speed** 30 knots + dived **Armament** 5 Torpedo Tubes **Complement** 116.

Notes
A follow-on class of ships from the Valiant Class. These submarines have an updated Sonar and Torpedo system. The Class are now based at Faslane (SOVEREIGN and SPLENDID will move to Faslane after their current refits). SWIFTSURE is awaiting disposal at Rosyth.

15

● OFFICIAL PHOTO

HMS Turbulent

TRAFALGAR CLASS

Ship	Pennant Number	Completion Date	Builder
TRENCHANT	S91	1989	Vickers
TALENT	S92	1990	Vickers
TRIUMPH	S93	1991	Vickers
TRAFALGAR	S107	1983	Vickers
TURBULENT	S110	1984	Vickers
TIRELESS	S117	1985	Vickers
TORBAY	S118	1986	Vickers

Displacement 4,500 tons **Dimensions** 85m x 10m x 8m **Speed** 30 + dived **Armament** 5 Torpedo Tubes **Complement** 125.

Notes
Enhanced development of the Swiftsure Class. Quieter, faster and with greater endurance than their predecessors. Design option studies into a new SSN (based upon the Trafalgar Class) have been announced. Orders are expected to be placed in the mid to late 90's.

HMS Unseen

UPHOLDER CLASS

Ship	Pennant Number	Completion Date	Builder
UPHOLDER	S40	1989	Vickers
UNSEEN	S41	1991	Cammell Laird
URSULA	S42	1992	Cammell Laird
UNICORN	S43	1993	Cammell Laird

Displacement 2,400 tons (dived) **Dimensions** 70m x 8m x 5m **Speed** 20 knots dived **Armament** 6 Torpedo Tubes: Sub Harpoon missile **Complement** 44.

Notes
A new class of conventionally powered submarines. UPHOLDER'S entry into service was delayed by industrial disputes and trials problems. Of 19 proposed vessels only the ships listed above have now been built. The first three boats of the Class to be completed are being taken in hand at Devonport to rectify defects in the torpedo firing system.

• HMS GANNET

HMS Oracle

OBERON CLASS

Ship	Pennant Number	Completion Date	Builder
ORACLE	S16	1963	C. Laird
OPOSSUM	S19	1964	C. Laird
OPPORTUNE	S20	1964	Scotts

Displacement 2,410 tons (submerged) **Dimensions** 90m x 8m x 5m **Speed** 12 knots surface, 17 knots submerged **Armament** 8 Torpedo Tubes **Complement** 70.

Notes

The remainder of this Class will be paid off by mid 1993 as the Upholder Class become operational. ONYX, now at Birkenhead is open daily to the public. OCELOT is at Chatham awaiting restoration for eventual public display. OSIRIS was sold to the Canadian Government in late 1992 for spares – but remains in the UK for dismantling.

18

OFFICIAL PHOTO

HMS Ark Royal

INVINCIBLE CLASS

Ship	Pennant Number	Completion Date	Builder
INVINCIBLE	R05	1979	Vickers
ILLUSTRIOUS	R06	1982	Swan Hunter
ARK ROYAL	R07	1985	Swan Hunter

Displacement 19,500 tons **Dimensions** 206m x 32m x 6.5m **Speed** 28 knots **Armament** Sea Dart Missile, 2 x 20mm guns, 3 Phalanx/Goalkeeper **Aircraft** 8 x Sea Harrier, 12 x Sea King **Complement** 900 + aircrews.

Notes
Manpower problems dictate that two ships are kept in the operational fleet, with the third being in refit or reserve. ILLUSTRIOUS is currently at Devonport but is expected to complete a lengthy refit during 1993.

HMS Fearless

FEARLESS CLASS

Ship	Pennant Number	Completion Date	Builder
FEARLESS	L10	1965	Harland & Wolff
INTREPID	L11	1967	J. Brown

Displacement 12,500 tons, 19,500 tons (flooded) **Dimensions** 158m x 24m x 8m **Speed** 20 knots **Armament** 2 Sea Cat Missile Systems, 2 x 40mm guns, 4 x 30mm + 2 x 20mm (INTREPID only) 2 x Vulcan Phalanx (FEARLESS only) **Complement** 580.

Notes

Multi-purpose ships that can operate helicopters for embarked Royal Marine Commandos. 4 landing craft are carried on an internal deck and are flooded out when the ship docks down. INTREPID paid off in 1991. She is unlikely to see further sea service and is in reserve at Portsmouth with a maintenance crew of approximately 90 men. A decision was made in late 1991 that both vessels would be replaced but it could be many years before any replacement vessel joins the Fleet. Thanks to their age both these ships have become extremely expensive to keep operational.

20

HMS Bristol

BRISTOL CLASS (Type 82)

Ship	Pennant Number	Completion Date	Builder
BRISTOL	D23	1972	Swan Hunter

Displacement 6,750 tons **Dimensions** 154m x 17m x 7m **Speed** 30 knots + **Armament** 1 x 4.5" gun, 1 Sea Dart Missile System, 4 x 30mm + 4 x 20mm guns **Complement** 407.

Notes
Four ships of this class were ordered but three later cancelled when requirement for large escorts for fixed wing aircraft carriers ceased to exist. Helicopter Deck provided but no aircraft normally carried. Fitted for, but not with, Vulcan Phalanx. Paid off in June 1991. She is expected to replace KENT as a harbour training ship for Sea Cadets at Portsmouth, once funding is secured.

DESTROYERS

21

● OFFICIAL PHOTO

SHEFFIELD CLASS
(Type 42) Batch 1 & 2

Ship	Pennant Number	Completion Date	Builder
BIRMINGHAM	D86	1976	C. Laird
NEWCASTLE	D87	1978	Swan Hunter
GLASGOW	D88	1978	Swan Hunter
EXETER	D89	1980	Swan Hunter
SOUTHAMPTON	D90	1981	Vosper T.
NOTTINGHAM	D91	1982	Vosper T.
LIVERPOOL	D92	1982	C. Laird
CARDIFF	D108	1979	Vickers

Displacement 3,660 tons **Dimensions** 125m x 15m x 7m **Speed** 29 knots **Armament** 1 x 1.4" gun, 4 x 20mm guns, Sea Dart Missile System: 2 x Phalanx, Lynx Helicopter, 6 Torpedo Tubes **Complement** 280 +.

Notes
Sister Ships SHEFFIELD and COVENTRY lost in 1982 during the Falklands conflict. All ships are to be modernised with new radar and electronic warfare systems. SOUTHAMPTON completed repairs during 1991 to damage inflicted during a Gulf collision and became operational again in 1992.

22

● OFFICIAL PHOTO

HMS Gloucester

SHEFFIELD CLASS
(Type 42) Batch 3

Ship	Pennant Number	Completion Date	Builder
MANCHESTER	D95	1983	Vickers
GLOUCESTER	D96	1984	Vosper T.
EDINBURGH	D97	1985	C. Laird
YORK	D98	1984	Swan Hunter

Displacement 4,775 tons **Dimensions** 132m x 15m x 7m **Speed** 30 knots + **Armament** 1 x 1.4" gun, 2 x Phalanx, 4 x 20mm guns. Sea Dart missile system. Lynx Helicopter, 6 Torpedo Tubes **Complement** 301.

Notes
"Stretched' versions of earlier ships of this class. Designed to provide area defence of a task force. Deck edge stiffening fitted to counter increased hull stress. EDINBURGH emerged from refit in late 1990 with new bow and forward mounted Phalanx. Studies continue on the future frigate requirement to replace these vessels – a collaborative venture with France is underway.

HMS Brilliant

BROADSWORD CLASS
(Type 22) Batch 1

Ship	Pennant Number	Completion Date	Builder
BROADSWORD	F88	1978	Yarrow
BATTLEAXE	F89	1980	Yarrow
BRILLIANT	F90	1981	Yarrow
BRAZEN	F91	1982	Yarrow

Displacement 3,860 tons **Dimensions** 131m x 15m x 6m **Speed** 29 knots **Armament** 4 Exocet Missiles, 2 Sea Wolf Missile Systems, 4 x 30mm guns, 2 or 4 x 20mm guns, 6 Torpedo Tubes, 2 Lynx Helicopters **Complement** 224.

Notes
Successor to the successful Leander Class. Although capable of carrying 2 helicopters, only 1 normally embarked. These ships have been refitted with additional accommodation and classroom facilities and deploy as Dartmouth Training Ships in a rota of two ships as a time.

24

HMS Coventry

BROADSWORD CLASS
(Type 22) Batch 2

Ship	Pennant Number	Completion Date	Builder
BOXER	F92	1983	Yarrow
BEAVER	F93	1984	Yarrow
BRAVE•	F94	1985	Yarrow
LONDON •	F95	1986	Yarrow
SHEFFIELD •	F96	1987	Swan Hunter
COVENTRY •	F98	1988	Swan Hunter

Displacement 4100 tons **Dimensions** 143m x 15m x 6m **Speed** 30 knots **Armament** 4 Exocet Missiles, 2 Sea Wolf Missile Systems, 4 x 30mm + 2 x 20mm guns, 6 Torpedo Tubes, 2 Lynx Helicopters **Complement** 273.

Notes
• Ships have enlarged hangar and flight deck. A Sea King can be, and is, carried in some ships of this class.

25

FRIGATES

HMS Cumberland

BROADSWORD CLASS
(Type 22) Batch 3

Ship	Pennant Number	Completion Date	Builder
CUMBERLAND	F85	1988	Yarrow
CAMPBELTOWN	F86	1988	C. Laird
CHATHAM	F87	1989	Swan Hunter
CORNWALL	F99	1987	Yarrow

Displacement 4,200 tons **Dimensions** 147m x 15m x 7m **Speed** 30 knots **Armament** 1 x 4.5" gun, 1 x Goalkeeper, 8 Harpoon, Seawolf, 4 x 30mm guns, 6 Torpedo Tubes, 2 Lynx or 1 Sea King Helicopter **Complement** 250.

Notes
General purpose gun and Goalkeeper system added to these ships as a direct result of lessons learned during Falklands conflict. All these ships have a major A/S and intelligence gathering capability. Cost £180 million each.

HMS Lancaster

DUKE CLASS (Type 23)

Ship	Pennant Number	Completion Date	Builder
LANCASTER	F229	1991	Yarrow
NORFOLK	F230	1989	Yarrow
ARGYLL	F231	1991	Yarrow
MARLBOROUGH	F233	1991	Swan Hunter
IRON DUKE	F234	1992	Yarrow
MONMOUTH	F235	1993	Yarrow
MONTROSE	F236	1993	Yarrow
WESTMINSTER	F237	Building	Swan Hunter
NORTHUMBERLAND	F238	Building	Swan Hunter
RICHMOND	F239	Building	Swan Hunter

Displacement 3,500 tons **Dimensions** 133m x 15m x 5m **Speed** 28 knots **Armament** Harpoon & Seawolf missile systems: 1 x 45" gun, 4 x 2 twin, magazine launched, Torpedo Tubes **Complement** 157.

Notes
Three further ships, SOMERSET (F240), GRAFTON (F241) and SUTHERLAND (F242) ordered during 1991.

HMS Andromeda

LEANDER CLASS
(Sea Wolf Conversions)

Ship	Pennant Number	Completion Date	Builder
ANDROMEDA	F57	1968	HM Dockyard Portsmouth
SCYLLA	F71	1970	HM Dockyard Devonport

Displacement 2,962 tons **Dimensions** 113m x 13m x 5m **Speed** 27 knots **Armament** Sea Wolf System, 4 x Exocet Missiles, 2 x 20mm guns, 6Torpedo Tubes, 1 Lynx helicopter **Complement** 260.

Notes
Having served the Fleet extremely well over 25 years the faithful Leander Class are rapidly leaving the active Fleet. ARIADNE was sold to Chile in 1992, HERMIONE and JUPITER paid off during 1992, JUNO paid off for disposal December 1992. ANDROMEDA will be placed in Reserve during 1993.

HMS Sirius

LEANDER CLASS
(Exocet Conversions)

Ship	Pennant Number	Completion Date	Builder
SIRIUS	F40	1966	HMD Porstmouth
ARGONAUT	F56	1967	Hawthorn Leslie

Displacement 2,860 tons **Dimensions** 113m x 12m x 5m **Speed** 27 knots **Armament** 4 Exocet Missiles, 3 Sea Cat Missile Systems, 2 x 40mm guns, 6 Torpedo Tubes, 1 Lynx helicopter **Complement** 230.

Notes
Ships have been refitted with Towed Array sonar and their armament reduced to 2 Sea Cat systems. Structural and mechanical problems are increasing the maintenance requirement for these elderly Leander class ships.

● HMS OSPREY

HMS Avenger

AMAZON CLASS
(Type 21)

Ship	Pennant Number	Completion Date	Builder
AMAZON	F169	1974	Vosper T.
ACTIVE	F171	1977	Vosper T.
AMBUSCADE	F172	1975	Yarrow
ARROW	F173	1976	Yarrow
ALACRITY	F174	1977	Yarrow
AVENGER	F185	1978	Yarrow

Displacement 3,250 tons **Dimensions** 117m x 13m x 6m **Speed** 30 knots **Armament** 1 x 4.5" gun, 2 x 20mm guns, 4 Exocet Missiles, 1 Sea Cat Missile System, 1 Lynx helicopter, 6 Torpedo Tubes **Complement** 170.

Notes

Sister ships ANTELOPE and ARDENT lost during the Falklands conflict. All 6 ships have been given extra hull strengthening. This class (built to a commercial design, and subsequently sold to the Ministry of Defence) have received no major mid-life modernisation. The first of this Class is expected to pay off for disposal in 1993 as further Type 23's join the active Fleet.

● OFFICIAL PHOTO

MINE COUNTERMEASURES SHIPS (MCMV'S) BRECON CLASS

Ship	Pennant Number	Completion Date	Builder
BRECON	1980	M29	Vosper T.
LEDBURY	1981	M30	Vosper T.
CATTISTOCK	1982	M31	Vosper T.
COTTESMORE	1983	M32	Yarrow
BROCKLESBY	1983	M33	Vosper T.
MIDDLETON	1984	M34	Yarrow
DULVERTON	1983	M35	Vosper T.
BICESTER	1986	M36	Vosper T.
CHIDDINGFOLD	1984	M37	Vosper T.
ATHERSTONE	1987	M38	Vosper T.
HURWORTH	1985	M39	Vosper T.
BERKELEY	1988	M40	Vosper T.
QUORN	1989	M41	Vosper T.

Displacement 625 tonnes **Dimensions** 60m x 10m x 2.2m **Speed** 17 knots **Armament** 1x30mm + 2 x 20mm guns **Complement** 45.

Notes
The largest warships ever built of glass reinforced plastic. Designed to replace the Coniston Class – their cost (£35m each) has dictated the size of the class. Very sophisticated ships – and lively seaboats! During 1992 some vessels were used in a Fishery Protection role.

31

M C M

V E S S E L S

HMS Carron

FLEET MINESWEEPERS
RIVER CLASS

Ship	Pennant Number	Completion Date	Builder
WAVENEY	M2003	1984	Richards
CARRON	M2004	1984	Richards
DOVEY	M2005	1984	Richards
HELFORD	M2006	1984	Richards
HUMBER	M2007	1985	Richards
BLACKWATER	M2008	1985	Richards
ITCHEN	M2009	1985	Richards
HELMSDALE	M2010	1985	Richards
ORWELL	M2011	1985	Richards
RIBBLE	M2012	1985	Richards
SPEY	M2013	1985	Richards
ARUN	M2014	1986	Richards

Displacement 850 tonnes **Dimensions** 47m x 10m x 3m **Speed** 14 knots **Armament** 1x40mm + 2 x GPMG **Complement** 30.

Notes
MCM ships serving with the RNR. BLACKWATER has an RN ships company and is in the FIshery Protection Squadron (FPS). Built to commercial specifications with steel hulls. Designed for 'sweeping in deep water', HELMSDALE and RIBBLE laid up (at Portsmouth) in 1991 as a defence economy. A Ministerial announcement was due in late 1992 regarding the entire future of the Royal Naval Reserve – subsequently the future of these ships is unclear.

● MARITIME PHOTOGRAPHIC

HMS Nurton

CONISTON CLASS

Ship	Pennant Number	Ship	Pennant Number
BRINTON	M1114	NURTON	M1166
WILTON	M1116	SHERATON	M1181
IVESTON ●	M1151	KELLINGTON ●	M1154

Displacement 425 tons **Dimensions** 46m x 9m x 3m **Speed** 15 knots **Armament** 1 x 40mm gun **Complement** 29/38.

Notes
120 of this class were built in the early 50s but most have now been sold overseas or scrapped. They have fulfilled many roles over the years and have given excellent service. WILTON, built of glassfibre in 1973, was the world's first 'plastic' warship. She is a training ship for BRNC Dartmouth. SOBERTON, the last true Minesweeper, paid off in 1992 for a static role with the Sea Cadet Corps at Erith. IVESTON and KELLINGTON are in reserve at Portsmouth. NURTON will be the last of the Class to remain in service.

HMS Walney

SANDOWN CLASS

Ship	Pennant Number	Completion Date	Builder
SANDOWN	M101	1989	Vosper T.
INVERNESS	M102	1991	Vosper T.
CROMER	M103	1991	Vosper T.
WALNEY	M104	1992	Vosper T.
BRIDPORT	M105	1993	Vosper T.

Displacement 450 tons **Dimensions** 53m x 10m x 2m **Speed** 13 knots **Armament** 1 x 30mm gun **Complement** 34.

Notes
A new class dedicated to a single mine hunting role. Propulsion is by vectored thrust and bow thrusters. Up to 15 more ships were planned, but the 7 due to be ordered in 1991 were cancelled. Six similar ships are being built for Saudi Arabia.

HMS Dumbarton Castle

CASTLE CLASS

Ship	Pennant Number	Completion Date	Builder
LEEDS CASTLE	P258	1981	Hall Russell
DUMBARTON CASTLE	P265	1982	Hall Russell

Displacement 1,450 tons **Dimensions** 81m x 11m x 3m **Speed** 20 knots **Armament** 1 x 40mm gun **Complement** 40.

Notes

These ships have a dual role – that of fishery protection and offshore patrols within the limits of UK territorial waters. Unlike the Island Class these ships are able to operate helicopters – including Sea King aircraft. Trials have been conducted to assess the suitability of these ships as Minelayers. DUMBARTON CASTLE currently on long term deployment to the Falklands Islands with her ships' company rotating every four months.

PATROL VESSELS

HMS Alderney

ISLAND CLASS

Ship	Pennant Number	Completion Date	Builder
ANGLESEY	P277	1979	Hall Russell
ALDERNEY	P278	1979	Hall Russell
JERSEY	P295	1976	Hall Russell
GUERNSEY	P297	1977	Hall Russell
SHETLAND	P298	1977	Hall Russell
ORKNEY	P299	1977	Hall Russell
LINDISFARNE	P300	1978	Hall Russell

Displacement 1,250 tons **Dimensions** 60m x 11m x 4m **Speed** 17 knots **Armament** 1 x 40mm gun **Complement** 39.

Notes
Built on trawler lines these ships were introduced to protect the extensive British interests in North Sea oil installations and to patrol the 200 mile fishery limit. The future of the Class depends upon the outcome of a review into the future role and composition of the Fishery Protection Squadron.

HMS Plover

PEACOCK CLASS

Ship	Pennant Number	Completion Date	Builder
PEACOCK	P239	1983	Hall Russell
PLOVER	P240	1983	Hall Russell
STARLING	P241	1984	Hall Russell

Displacement 700 tons **Dimensions** 60m x 10m x 5m **Speed** 28 knots **Armament** 1 x 76mm gun **Complement** 31.

Notes

The first warships to carry the 76mm Oto Melara gun. They are used to provide an ocean going back-up to the Marine Department of the Hong Kong Police. The Government of Hong Kong has paid 75% of the building and maintenance costs of these vessels. Sister ships SWALLOW and SWIFT returned to UK in 1988 and were sold (Oct 88) to the Irish Navy after only 3 years RN service. All three vessels are expected to remain in Hong Kong until 1997.

37

● P. DAVIES

HMS Archer

COASTAL TRAINING CRAFT
ARCHER CLASS

Ship	Pennant Number	Completion Date	Builder
ARCHER	P264	1985	Watercraft
BITER	P270	1985	Watercraft
SMITER	P272	1986	Watercraft
PURSUER	P273	1988	Vosper
BLAZER	P279	1988	Vosper
DASHER	P280	1988	Vosper
PUNCHER	P291	1988	Vosper
CHARGER	P292	1988	Vosper
RANGER	P293	1988	Vosper
TRUMPETER	P294	1988	Vosper

Displacement 43 tonnes **Dimensions** 20m x 6m x 1m **Speed** 20 knots **Armament** Nil **Complement** 14.

Notes

In service with RNR divisions and RN University units. TRUMPETER and RANGER deployed to Gibraltar in 1991.

● LA PHOT BALL

HMS Cygnet

BIRD CLASS

Ship	Pennant Number	Completion Date	Builder
REDPOLE	P259	1970	Fairmile
KINGFISHER	P260	1975	R. Dunston
CYGNET	P261	1976	R. Dunston

Displacement 190 tons **Dimensions** 37m x 7m x 2m **Speed** 21 knots **Complement** 24.

Notes
REDPOLE commissioned into the Royal Navy in 1985 after service as an RAF search and rescue craft.

39

● R.M. POOLE

HMS Messina

MESSINA CLASS

Ship	Pennant Number	Completion Date	Builder
MESSINA	A107	1982	R. Dunston

Displacement 127 tons **Dimensions** 25m x 6m x 2m **Speed** 10 knots **Complement** 9/13.

Notes

Very similar to the RMAS/RNXS tenders. MESSINA is a training ship for Royal Marines based at Poole. IXWORTH (A318), IRONBRIDGE (A311) and DATCHET (A357) are all former RMAS tenders now flying the White/Blue Ensign as diving tenders. DATCHET for disposal in mid 1993.

HMS Roebuck

ROEBUCK CLASS

Ship	Pennant Number	Completion Date	Builder
ROEBUCK	A130	1986	Brooke Marine

Displacement 1500 tonnes **Dimensions** 64m x 13m x 4m **Speed** 15 knots **Complement** 47.

Notes

Was due to replace HECLA in the Survey fleet until the latter reprieved in 1987 for further service. Fitted with the latest fixing aids and sector scanning sonar. A chartered commercial vessel is expected to join the Survey Fleet during 1993.

HMS Herald

HECLA CLASS

Ship	Pennant Number	Completion Date	Builder
HECLA	A133	1965	Yarrow
HERALD	A138	1974	Robb Caledon

Displacement 2,733 tons **Dimensions** 79m x 15m x 5m **Speed** 14 knots **Complement** 115.

Notes

Able to operate for long periods away from shore support, these ships and the smaller ships of the Hydrographic Fleet collect the data that is required to produce the Admiralty Charts and publications which are sold to mariners worldwide. HERALD is an improved version of the earlier ships. HECATE remains (late 1992) for sale at Portsmouth.

● OFFICIAL PHOTO

HMS Bulldog

BULLDOG CLASS

Ship	Pennant Number	Completion Date	Builder
BULLDOG	A317	1968	Brooke Marine
BEAGLE	A319	1968	Brooke Marine

Displacement 1,088 tons **Dimensions** 60m x 11m x 4m **Speed** 15 knots **Complement** 39.

Notes
Designed to operate in coastal waters. Both have been extensively refitted to extend hull life. FOX was sold for commercial service in December 1988. FAWN sold for commercial service as M/V RED FULMAR
GLEANER (A86) is a small inshore survey craft based at Portsmouth.

HMS Challenger

SEABED OPERATIONS VESSEL

Ship	Pennant Number	Completion Date	Builder
CHALLENGER	K07	1984	Scott Lithgow

Displacement 6,400 tons **Dimensions** 134m x 18m x 5m **Speed** 15 knots **Complement** 185.

Notes

CHALLENGER was equipped to find, inspect and, where appropriate, recover objects from the seabed at greater depths than is currently possible. She was designed with a saturation diving system enabling up to 12 men to live in comfort for long periods in a decompression chamber amidships, taking their turns to be lowered in a diving bell to work on the seabed. Also fitted to carry out salvage work. Paid off in November 1990 as a defence economy. No suitable buyer has been found and discussions continue regarding her future. All saturation diving systems have now been removed from the vessel.

● OFFICIAL PHOTO

HMY Britannia

ROYAL YACHT

Ship	Pennant Number	Completion Date	Builder
BRITANNIA	A00	1954	J. Brown

Displacement 5,280 tons **Dimensions** 126m x 17m x 5m **Speed** 21 knots **Complement** 250.

Notes
Probably the best known ship in the Royal Navy, BRITANNIA was designed to be converted to a hospital ship in time of war but this conversion was not made during the Falklands or Gulf crisis. Is available for use in NATO exercises when not on 'Royal' business. Normally to be seen in Portsmouth Harbour when not away on official duties. The only seagoing ship in the RN commanded by an Admiral.

HMS Endurance

ICE PATROL SHIP

Ship	Pennant Number	Completion Date	Builder
ENDURANCE	A171	1990	Ulstein-Hatlo

Displacement 5,129 tons **Dimensions** 91m x 17.9m x 6.5m **Speed** 14.9 knots **Armament** Small arms **Aircraft** 2 Lynx **Complement** 113.

Notes
Charatered for only 7 months in late 1991 to replace the older vessel of the same name. Originally M/V POLAR CIRCLE, renamed HMS POLAR CIRCLE (A176) and then purchased by MOD(N) and renamed again in October 1992 to current name.

HMS Boxer

HMS Marlborough

HMS Fearless

HM Ships Invincible, Norfolk and Boxer

HMY Brittania

RFA Fort Victoria

THE ROYAL FLEET AUXILIARY

The Royal Fleet Auxiliary Service (RFA) is a civilian manned fleet owned and operated by the Ministry of Defence. Its main task is to supply warships of the Royal Navy at sea with fuel, food, stores and ammunition which they need to remain operational while away from base. With so few bases overseas which can be guaranteed in time of tension – let alone during any conflict – it has become vital, over the years, that everything from the smallest nut and bolt to a complete aero engine is taken on any naval deployment away from our coasts. The lack of that nut and bolt could well stop a ship in its tracks – literally. Increasingly, the service also provides aviation support for the Royal Navy – together with amphibious support and secure sea transport for army units and their equipment.

With a Navy rapidly shrinking in size – and with more reductions planned – it is inevitable that economies in size are being investigated within the service. In recent years vessels have paid off – or been reduced to reserve. Support ships are, however, vital if British Forces are to be supported at any distance from our shores.

With the new Fort class eventually coming into service it is difficult to see how small "single ship" overseas operations are to be supported by the RFA. It is inconceivable to think one of these huge vessels being sent to support a single frigate/destroyer in the Falklands or West Indies. With such huge ships in the RFA service these days, the eggs are very much "going into one basket" which may just be acceptable until the "baskets" need to be refitted…With a smaller Navy the RFA urgently needs smaller, cost effective vessels in greater numbers than are currently planned. It would be comforting to know that such vessels may be available to charter in an emergency but the size and shape of the British Merchant service still gives cause for considerable concern. As from 1st April 1993 the command and control of the RFA service will move from its traditional RNSTS (Civil Service) management to a different structure under the direct control of C in C Fleet. It would seem to make a lot more sense…

SHIPS OF THE ROYAL FLEET AUXILIARY
Pennant Numbers

Ship	Pennant Number	Ship	Pennant Number	Ship	Pennant Number
BRAMBLELEAF	A81	ARGUS	A135	FORT GEORGE	A388
BAYLEAF	A109	GREY ROVER	A269	RESOURCE	A480
ORANGELEAF	A110	BLUE ROVER	A270	SIR BEDIVERE	L3004
OAKLEAF	A111	GOLD ROVER	A271	SIR GALAHAD	L3005
OLWEN	A122	BLACK ROVER	A273	SIR GERAINT	L3027
OLNA	A123	FORT GRANGE	A385	SIR PERCIVALE	L3036
OLMEDA	A124	FORT AUSTIN	A386	SIR TRISTRAM	L3505
DILIGENCE	A132	FORT VICTORIA	A387		

A number of merchant ships are on charter to various MOD departments. They include MAERSK GANNET, MAERSK ASCENCION, ST BRANDAN, INDOMITABLE & OIL MARINER & in support of the Falkland Island commitment. NORTHELLA, PROUD SEAHORSE, BRITISH ENTERPRISE IV, MARINE EXPLORER and NORTHERN HORIZON have hydrographic, training/trials roles in UK waters.

RFA Olwen

'OL' CLASS

Ship	Pennant Number	Completion Date	Builder
OLWEN	A122	1965	Hawthorn Leslie
OLNA	A123	1966	Hawthorn Leslie
OLMEDA	A124	1965	Swan Hunter

Displacement 36,000 tons **Dimensions** 197m x 26m x 10m **Speed** 19 knots **Complement** 92.

Notes

These ships can operate up to 3 Sea King helicopters. Dry stores can be carried – and transferred at sea – as well as a wide range of fuel, aviation spirit and lubricants. All these vessels have now been refitted to bring them up to modern standards – and to increase their 'lifespan' – possibly to the turn of the century.

RFA Gold Rover

ROVER CLASS

Ship	Pennant Number	Completion Date	Builder
GREY ROVER	A269	1970	Swan Hunter
BLUE ROVER	A270	1970	Swan Hunter
GOLD ROVER	A271	1974	Swan Hunter
BLACK ROVER	A273	1974	Swan Hunter

Displacement 11,522 tons **Dimensions** 141m x 19m x 7m **Speed** 18 knots **Armament** 2 x 20mm guns **Complement** 49/54

Notes
Small Fleet Tankers designed to supply HM ships with fresh water, dry cargo and refrigerated provisions as well as a range of fuel and lubricants. Helicopter deck but no hangar. GREEN ROVER sold to Indonesia 1992.

TANKERS

59

RFA Bayleaf

LEAF CLASS

Ship	Pennant Number	Completion Date	Builder
BRAMBLELEAF	A81	1980	Cammell Laird
BAYLEAF	A109	1982	Cammell Laird
ORANGELEAF	A110	1982	Cammell Laird
OAKLEAF	A111	1981	Uddevalla

Displacement 37,747 tons **Dimensions** 170m x 26m x 12m **Speed** 14.5 knots **Complement** 60.

Notes
All are ex merchant ships. BRAMBLELEAF is owned by MOD (N), the remainder are on bare boat charter. OAKLEAF (ex OKTANIA) differs from the other ships of the class which are all commercial Stat 32 tankers. At 49,310 tons she is the largest vessel in RFA/RN service. APPLELEAF taken over by the Royal Australian Navy (as HMAS Westralia) in late 1989 – on a 5 years charter – with an option to purchase.

RFA Fort Grange

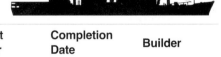

FORT CLASS I

Ship	Pennant Number	Completion Date	Builder
FORT GRANGE	A385	1978	Scott Lithgow
FORT AUSTIN	A386	1979	Scott Lithgow

Displacement 23,384 tons **Dimensions** 183m x 24m x 9m **Speed** 20 knots **Complement** 201, (120 RFA, 36 RNSTS & 45 RN).

Notes
Full hangar and maintenance facilities are provided and up to four Sea King helicopters can be carried for both the transfer of stores and anti-submarine protection of a group of ships. Both ships can be armed with 4 x 20mm guns mounted on the Scot platforms. Both are fitted with 3" Chaff Systems.

61

STORE SHIPS

RFA Fort Victoria

FORT CLASS II

Ship	Pennant Number	Completion Date	Builder
FORT VICTORIA	A387	1992	Harland & Wolff
FORT GEORGE	A388	Building	Swan Hunter

Displacement 31,500 tons **Dimensions** 204m x 30m x 9m **Speed** 20 knots **Armament** 4 x 30mm guns, Sea Wolf Missile System **Complement** 100 (RFA), 24 civilians, 32 RN and up to 112 aircrew.

Notes
These ships can operate 3 Sea King helicopters. A "one stop" replenishment ship with the widest range of armaments, fuel and spares carried. Maintenance facilities for helicopters onboard. Delays at the builder resulted in the plans for FORT VICTORIA to enter service in 1992 being abandoned. It is hoped she will enter service in 1993 – her sister ship 12 months later..

● OFFICIAL PHOTO

RFA Resource

REGENT CLASS

Ship	Pennant Number	Completion Date	Builder
RESOURCE	A480	1967	Scotts

Displacement 22,890 tons **Dimensions** 195m x 24m x 8m **Speed** 21 knots
Armament 2 x 20mm guns **Complement** 182, (RFA 112, RNSTS 37, RN 11).

Notes
The widest range of naval armament stores are carried onboard plus a limited range of
general naval stores and food. When the Wessex 5 was withdrawn from service in April
1987 both ships lost their permanently embarked helicopter but they retain full flight
deck facilities. RESOURCE reverted to Reserve (Preservation by Operation) status at
Rosyth in November 1991 but brought forward in late 1992 for service in the Adriatic.
REGENT for sale late 1992.

● OFFICIAL PHOTO

RFA Sir Galahad

LANDING SHIPS
SIR LANCELOT CLASS

Ship	Pennant Number	Completion Date	Builder
SIR BEDIVERE	L3004	1967	Hawthorn
SIR GALAHAD	L3005	1987	Swan Hunter
SIR GERAINT	L3027	1967	Stephen
SIR PERCIVALE	L3036	1968	Hawthorn
SIR TRISTRAM	L3505	1967	Hawthorn

Displacement 5,550 tons **Dimensions** 126m x 18m x 4m **Speed** 17 knots **Armament** Can be fitted with 2 x 40mm guns in emergency **Complement** 65, SIR GALAHAD (8,451 tons. 140m x 20m **Complement** 58).

Notes
Manned by the RFA but tasked by the Army, these ships are used for heavy secure transport of stores – embarked by bow and stern doors – and beach assault landings. Can operate helicopters from tank deck if required. SIR LANCELOT sold for commercial service as a seagoing casino at Capetown in 1989.

64

RFA Diligence

Ship	Pennant Number	Completion Date	Builder
DILIGENCE	A132	1981	Oresundsvarvet

Displacement 5,814 tons **Dimensions** 120m x 12m x 3m **Speed** 15 knots **Armament** 2 x 20mm **Complement** RFA 40. RN Personnel – approx 100.

Notes

Formerly the M/V Stena Inspector purchased (£25m) for service in the South Atlantic. Accommodation is provided for a 100 man Fleet Maintenance Unit. Her deep diving complex was removed and workshops added. Has given valuable support to a wide range of warships in the Falklands and Gulf.

RFA Argus

Ship	Pennant Number	Completion Date	Builder
ARGUS	A135	1981	Cantieri Navali Breda

Displacement 28,081 tons (full load) **Dimensions** 175m x 30m x 8m **Speed** 18 knots **Armament** 4 x 30mm, 2 x 20mm **Complement** 254 (inc 137 Air Group) **Aircraft** 6 Sea King, 12 Harriers can be carried in a "ferry role".

Notes

Formerly the M/V CONTENDER BEZANT taken up from trade during the Falklands crisis. Purchased in 1984 (£13 million) for conversion to an 'Aviation Training Ship'. A £50 million re-build was undertaken at Belfast from 1984-87. Undertook rapid conversion in October 1990 to "Primary Casualty Reception Ship" (Hospital Ship!) for service in the Gulf. These facilities remain "mothballed" on board for activation if required.

ROYAL MARITIME
AUXILIARY SERVICE

The Royal Maritime Auxiliary Service Fleet is administered by the Director of Marine Services (Naval) to whom the Captains of the Ports and Resident Naval Officers at the various Naval Bases are mainly responsible for the provision of Marine Services to the Royal Navy. The Fleet continues to be reduced as the size of the Royal Navy has itself shrunk. It is still however responsible for over 400 hulls ranging from ocean going ships to small harbour lighters. The Fleet also includes 13 Army Range safety craft, 13 RAF Maritime Craft and over 40 MOD Police boats.

Ships of the RMAS, which can be seen at work in all the Naval Bases throughout the United Kingdom and at Gibraltar, are easily identified by their black hulls, buff coloured superstructure and funnels, and by the RMAS flag, which is a blue ensign defaced in the fly by a yellow anchor over two wavy lines. Pennant numbers are painted only on those vessels that are normally employed outside harbour limits.

● F.GEORGE

SHIPS OF
THE ROYAL MARITIME AUXILIARY SERVICE
Pennant Numbers

Ship	Pennant Number	Ship	Pennant Number
CAMERON	A72	LABRADOR	A168
MELTON	A83	KITTY	A170
MENAI	A84	LESLEY	A172
MEON	A87	LILAH	A174
MILFORD	A91	MARY	A175
ALSATIAN	A106	EDITH	A177
FELICITY	A112	HUSKY	A178
MAGNET	A114	MASTIFF	A180
LODESTONE	A115	IRENE	A181
CAIRN	A126	SALUKI	A182
TORRENT	A127	ISABEL	A183
DALMATIAN	A129	SALMOOR	A185
TORNADO	A140	SALMASTER	A186
TORCH	A141	SALMAID	A187
TORMENTOR	A142	POINTER	A188
TOREADOR	A143	SETTER	A189
WATERMAN	A146	JOAN	A190
FRANCES	A147	JOYCE	A193
FIONA	A148	GWENDOLINE	A196
FLORENCE	A149	SEALYHAM	A197
GENEVIEVE	A150	HELEN	A198
GEORGINA	A152	MYRTLE	A199
EXAMPLE	A153	SPANIEL	A201
EXPLORER	A154	NANCY	A202
DEERHOUND	A155	NORAH	A205
DAPHNE	A156	LLANDOVERY	A207
LOYAL HELPER	A157	LAMLASH	A208
SUPPORTER	A158	LECHLADE	A211
LOYAL WATCHER	A159	BEE	A216
LOYAL VOLUNTEER	A160	LOYAL MODERATOR	A220
LOYAL MEDIATOR	A161	FORCEFUL	A221
ELKHOUND	A162	NIMBLE	A222
EXPRESS	A163	POWERFUL	A223
GOOSANDER	A164	ADEPT	A224
POCHARD	A165	BUSTLER	A225
KATHLEEN	A166	CAPABLE	A226
EXPLOIT	A167	CAREFUL	A227

Ship	Pennant Number	Ship	Pennant Number
FAITHFUL	A228	KINTERBURY	A378
CRICKET	A229	CRICKLADE	A381
COCKCHAFER	A230	ARROCHAR	A382
DEXTEROUS	A231	APPLEBY	A383
ADAMANT	A232	CLOVELLY	A389
GNAT	A239	CRICCIETH	A391
SHEEPDOG	A250	GLENCOE	A392
LYDFORD	A251	DUNSTER	A393
LADYBIRD	A253	FINTRY	A394
MEAVEY	A254	GRASMERE	A402
CICALA	A263	CROMARTY	A488
SCARAB	A272	DORNOCH	A490
AURICULA	A285	ROLLICKER	A502
ILCHESTER	A308	HEADCORN	A1766
INSTOW	A309	HEVER	A1767
FOXHOUND	A326	HARLECH	A1768
BASSET	A327	HAMBLEDON	A1769
COLLIE	A328	LOYAL CHANCELLOR	A1770
CORGI	A330	LOYAL PROCTOR	A1771
FOTHERBY	A341	HOLMWOOD	A1772
IMPULSE	A344	HORNING	A1773
IMPETUS	A345	WATERSPOUT	Y19
FELSTED	A348	OILPRESS	Y21
ELKSTONE	A353	OILSTONE	Y22
EPWORTH	A355	OILWELL	Y23
ROYSTERER	A361	OILBIRD	Y25
DENMEAD	A363	OILMAN	Y26
WHITEHEAD	A364	WATERCOURSE	Y30
FULBECK	A365	WATERFOWL	Y31
ROBUST	A366	MOORHEN	Y32
NEWTON	A367	MOORFOWL	Y33
WARDEN	A368		

● I. BIGNELL

RMAS Roysterer

ROYSTERER CLASS

G.R.T. 1,036 tons **Dimensions** 54m x 12m x 6m **Speed** 15 knots **Complement** 21.

Notes
Built for salvage and long range towage, a role they only fulfil infrequently. They are, however, used for various "deepwater" trials for MOD research departments. ROBUST is due back into service in early 1993 after a period of lay-up/engine repairs.

TUGS

RMAS Impulse

IMPULSE CLASS

Ship	Pennant Number	Completion Date	Builder
IMPULSE	A344	1993	Dunston
IMPETUS	A345	1993	Dunston

G.R.T. 400 tons approx **Dimensions** 33m x 10m x 4m **Speed** 12 knots **Complement** 5.

Notes

These two new tugs are due for completion in mid 1993 and will serve as berthing tugs for the Trident Class submarines at Faslane. Until delivered a commercial tug (FLYING SPINDRIFT) has been chartered.

● I. BIGNELL

RMAS Adept

HARBOUR TUGS
TWIN UNIT TRACTOR TUGS (TUTT'S)

Ship	Pennant Number	Completion Date	Builder
FORCEFUL	A221	1985	R. Dunston
NIMBLE	A222	1985	R. Dunston
POWERFUL	A223	1985	R. Dunston
ADEPT	A224	﹨ 1980	R. Dunston
BUSTLER	A225	1981	R. Dunston
CAPABLE	A226	1981	R. Dunston
CAREFUL	A227	1982	R. Dunston
FAITHFUL	A228	1985	R. Dunston
DEXTEROUS	A231	1986	R. Dunston

G.R.T. 375 tons **Dimensions** 39m x 10m x 4m **Speed** 12 knots **Complement** 9.

Notes
The principal harbour tug in naval service. CAPABLE is at Gibraltar.

RMAS Foxhound

DOG CLASS

Ship	Pennant Number	Ship	Pennant Number
ALSATIAN	A106	POINTER	A188
CAIRN ●	A126	SETTER	A189
DALMATIAN	A129	SEALYHAM	A197
DEERHOUND	A155	SPANIEL	A201
ELKHOUND	A162	SHEEPDOG	A250
LABRADOR	A168	FOXHOUND	A326
HUSKY	A178	BASSET	A327
MASTIFF	A180	COLLIE ●	A328
SALUKI	A182	CORGI	A330

G.R.T. 152 tons **Dimensions** 29m x 8m x 4m **Speed** 12 knots **Complement** 5.

Notes

General harbour tugs – all completed between 1962 and 1972.

● No longer tugs. Refitted as trials vessels for service at Kyle of Lochalsh.

At least one of this class will be discarded once the new Impetus Class tugs are in service.

● C. HOCKADAY

RMAS Daphne

IMPROVED GIRL CLASS

Ship	Pennant Number	Ship	Pennant Number
DAPHNE	A156	EDITH	A177

G.R.T. 75 tons **Speed** 10 knots **Complement** 4.

Notes

All completed 1971-2. DAISY, DORIS, CHARLOTTE and CHRISTINE sold 1989 and DOROTHY in 1990. Both vessels will run on until they are uneconomical to maintain. There are no plans to replace them.

RMAS Kitty

IRENE CLASS

Ship	Pennant Number	Ship	Pennant Number
KATHLEEN	A166	ISABEL	A183
KITTY	A170	JOAN	A190
LESLEY	A172	JOYCE	A193
LILAH	A174	MYRTLE	A199
MARY	A175	NANCY	A202
IRENE	A181	NORAH	A205

G.R.T. 89 tons **Speed** 8 knots **Complement** 4.

Notes
Known as Water Tractors these craft are used for basin moves and towage of light barges.

● M.J. GASTON   **RMAS Felicity**

FELICITY CLASS

Ship	Pennant Number	Ship	Pennant Number
FELICITY	A112	GENEVIEVE	A150
FRANCES	A147	GEORGINA	A152
FIONA	A148	GWENDOLINE	A196
FLORENCE	A149	HELEN	A198

G.R.T. 80 tons **Speed** 10 knots **Complement** 4.

Notes
Water Tractors – completed in 1973; FRANCES, FLORENCE and GENEVIEVE completed 1980.

RMAS Newton

RESEARCH VESSEL

Ship	Pennant Number	Completion Date	Builder
NEWTON	A367	1976	Scotts

G.R.T. 2,779 tons **Dimensions** 99m x 16m x 6m **Speed** 15 knots **Complement** 39

Notes
An underwater research vessel with a limited cable laying capability.
The Trials ship RMAS WHITEHEAD (A364) was for sale in late 1992.

TRIALS SHIPS

RMAS Auricula

TEST & EXPERIMENTAL SONAR TENDER

Ship	Pennant Number	Completion Date	Builder
AURICULA	A285	1981	Ferguson Bros

G.R.T. 981 tons **Dimensions** 52m x 11m x 3m **Speed** 12 knots **Complement** 20.

Notes
Employed on evaluation work of new sonar equipment that may equip RN ships of the future. Based as Portland. A reducing workload for this vessel casts some doubt regarding its future employment.

RMAS Arrochar

ARMAMENT STORES CARRIERS

Ship	Pennant Number	Completion Date	Builder
KINTERBURY	A378	1980	Appledore SB
ARROCHAR	A382	1981	Appledore SB

G.R.T. 1,357 tons **Dimensions** 64m x 12m x 5m **Speed** 14 knots **Complement** 19.

Notes
2 holds carry Naval armament stores, ammunition and guided missiles. Both vessels vary slightly. ARROCHAR (ex ST GEORGE) taken over in late 1988 from the Army. Both vessels are now operational and will be for about 2 years. One will then return to reserve at Portsmouth.

RMAS Cockchafer

INSECT CLASS

Ship	Pennant Number	Completion Date	Builder
BEE	A216	1970	C.D. Holmes
CRICKET	A229	1972	Beverley
COCKCHAFER	A230	1971	Beverley
GNAT	A239	1972	Beverley
LADYBIRD	A253	1973	Beverley
CICALA	A263	1971	Beverley
SCARAB	A272	1973	Beverley

G.R.T. 279 tons **Dimensions** 34m x 8m x 3m **Speed** 10.5 knots **Complement** 7-9.

Notes
CRICKET and SCARAB are fitted as Mooring Vessels and COCKCHAFER as a Trials Stores Carrier – remainder are Naval Armament carriers.

• C. HOCKADAY

XSV Loyal Chancellor

LOYAL CLASS

Ship	Pennant Number	Ship	Pennant Number
XSV LOYAL HELPER	A157	XSV LOYAL MEDIATOR	A161
XSV SUPPORTER	A158	XSV LOYAL MODERATOR	A220
XSV LOYAL WATCHER	A159	XSV LOYAL CHANCELLOR	A1770
XSV LOYAL VOLUNTEER	A160	XSV LOYAL PROCTOR	A1771

G.R.T. 112 tons **Dimensions** 24m x 6m x 3m **Speed** 10.5 knots **Complement** 24.

Notes

All these craft are operated by the Royal Naval Auxiliary Service (RNXS) – men (and women) – who, in time of emergency, would man these craft for duties as port control vessels. The whole future of the RNXS is under consideration within the MoD – hence the future of these vessels in unclear.

**T
E
N
D
E
R
S**

RMAS Adamant

ADAMANT

Ship	Pennant Number	Completion Date	Builder
ADAMANT	A232	1992	FBM (Cowes)

Displacement 170 tonnes GRT **Dimensions** 30m x 8m x 1m **Speed** 22 knots **Complement** 5

Notes
Twin catamaran hulls based on the commercial Red Jet design (as used by Red Funnel Ferry Co). First water jet propulsion vessel in the RMAS. For service as a Clyde personnel ferry.

• W. SARTORI

RMAS Horning

(TYPE A, B & X) TENDERS

Ship	Pennant Number	Ship	Pennant Number
MELTON	A83	CRICKLADE	A381
MENAI	A84	CLOVELLY	A389
MEON	A87	CRICCIETH	A391
MILFORD	A91	GLENCOE	A392
LLANDOVERY	A207	DUNSTER	A393
LAMLASH	A208	FINTRY	A394
LECHLADE	A211	GRASMERE	A402
LYDFORD	A251	CROMARTY	A488
ILCHESTER •	A308	DORNOCH	A490
INSTOW •	A309	HEADCORN	A1766
FOTHERBY	A341	HEVER	A1767
FELSTED	A348	HARLECH	A1768
ELKSTONE	A353	HAMBLEDON	A1769
EPWORTH	A355	HOLMWOOD	A1772
FULBECK	A365	HORNING	A1773

G.R.T. 78 tons **Dimensions** 24m x 6m x 3m **Speed** 10.5 knots **Complement** 4/5.

Notes

All completed since 1971 to replace Motor Fishing Vessels. Vessels marked • are diving tenders. Remainder are Training Tenders, Passenger Ferries, or Cargo Vessels. GLENCOE to RNR at Southampton 1991. FROXFIELD for sale late 1992. DENMEAD has been transferred to the RNR at Belfast. MEAVEY now operates for HMS SULTAN – as SULTAN VENTURER •, FOTHERBY for disposal mid 1993.

XSV Express

COASTAL TRAINING CRAFT
EXAMPLE CLASS

Ship	Pennant Number	Completion Date	Builder
XSV EXAMPLE	A153	1985	Watercraft
XSV EXPLORER	A154	1985	Watercraft
XSV EXPRESS	A163	1988	Vosper T
XSV EXPLOIT	A167	1988	Vosper T

Displacement 43 tons **Dimensions** 20m x 6m x 1m **Speed** 20 knots **Armament** Nil
Complement 14

Notes
Training vessels for the RNXS. In wartime would be used within ports/anchorages on port control duties.

● C. HOCKADAY

RMAS Oilwell

COASTAL OILERS
OILPRESS CLASS

Ship	Pennant Number	Completion Date	Builder
OILPRESS	Y21	1969	Appledore Shipbuilders
OILSTONE	Y22	1969	Appledore Shipbuilders
OILWELL	Y23	1969	Appledore Shipbuilders
OILBIRD	Y25	1969	Appledore Shipbuilders
OILMAN	Y26	1969	Appledore Shipbuilders

G.R.T. 362 tons **Dimensions** 41m x 9m x 3m **Speed** 11 knots **Complement** 5.

Notes
Employed as Harbour and Coastal Oilers. OILSTONE for disposal.

RMAS Watercourse

WATER CARRIERS
WATER CLASS

Ship	Pennant Number	Completion Date	Builder
WATERSPOUT	Y19	1967	Drypool Eng Co
WATERCOURSE	Y30	1974	Drypool Eng Co
WATERFOWL	Y31	1974	Drypool Eng Co
WATERMAN	A146	1978	R. Dunston

G.R.T. 263 tons **Dimensions** 40m x 8m x 2m **Speed** 11 knots **Complement** 5.

Notes
Capable of coastal passages, these craft normally supply either demineralised or fresh water to the Fleet within port limits. WATERSHED sold to Malta October 1992.

86

RMAS Lodestone

DEGAUSSING VESSELS
MAGNET CLASS

Ship	Pennant Number	Completion Date	Builder
MAGNET	A114	1979	Cleland
LODESTONE	A115	1980	Cleland

G.R.T. 828 tons **Dimensions** 55m x 12m x 4m **Speed** 14 knots **Complement** 9.

Notes
LODESTONE is currently operational (on the Clyde). MAGNET in reserve (Portsmouth).

RMAS Torrent

TORPEDO RECOVERY VESSELS (TRV'S)
TORRID CLASS

Ship	Pennant Number	Completion Date	Builder
TORRENT	A127	1971	Cleland SB Co

G.R.T. 550 tons **Dimensions** 46m x 9m x 3m **Speed** 12 knots **Complement** 14.

Notes
A stern ramp is built for the recovery of torpedoes fired for trials and exercises. A total of 32 can be carried.

RMAS Toreador

TORNADO CLASS

Ship	Pennant Number	Completion Date	Builder
TORNADO	A140	1979	Hall Russell
TORCH	A141	1980	Hall Russell
TORMENTOR	A142	1980	Hall Russell
TOREADOR	A143	1980	Hall Russell

G.R.T. 560 tons **Dimensions** 47m x 8m x 3m **Speed** 14 knots **Complement** 13.

Notes

TORCH is based at Portland, TORMENTOR at Plymouth – remainder on the Clyde. All vessels have had suitable rails fitted to enable them to operate as exercise minelayers.

RMAS Salmoor

MOORING & SALVAGE VESSELS
SAL CLASS

Ship	Pennant Number	Completion Date	Builder
SALMOOR	A185	1985	Hall Russell
SALMASTER	A186	1986	Hall Russell
SALMAID	A187	1986	Hall Russell

Displacement 2200 tonnes **Dimensions** 77m x 15m x 4m **Speed** 15 knots **Complement** 17.

Notes
Multi-purpose vessels designed to lay and maintain underwater targets and moorings and undertake a wide range of salvage tasks.

RMAS Goosander

WILD DUCK CLASS

Ship	Pennant Number	Completion Date	Builder
GOOSANDER	A164	1973	Robb Caledon

G.R.T. 900 tons* **Dimensions** 58mm x 12m x 4m **Speed** 10 knots **Complement** 18.

Notes

Capable of carrying out a wide range of duties laying moorings and heavy lift salvage work. 200 tons can be lifted over the bow. POCHARD is in reserve at Portsmouth but unlikely to see further service as she is being used as a source of spares to keep GOOSANDER operational.

91

● C. HOCKADAY

RMAS Moorhen

MOOR CLASS

Ship	Pennant Number	Completion Date	Builder
MOORHEN	Y32	1989	McTay Marine
MOORFOWL	Y33	1989	McTay Marine
CAMERON	A72	1991	Richard Dunston

Displacement 518 tons **Dimensions** 32m x 11m x 2m **Speed** 8 knots
Complement 10

Notes
Powered mooring lighters for use within sheltered coastal waters. (MOORHEN at Portsmouth, MOORFOWL at Devonport). CAMERON is similar but is employed as an Underwater Trials & Experimental vessel at Rosyth.

● C. HOCKADAY

RMAS Warden

WARDEN CLASS

Ship	Pennant Number	Completion Date	Builder
WARDEN	A368	1989	Richards

Displacement 626 tons **Dimensions** 48m x 10m x 4m **Speed** 15 knots **Complement** 11.

Notes
Accepted into service Nov 1989 to replace DOLWEN as the Range Mooring Vessel for RAE Aberporth (S. Wales). Based at Pembroke Dock. Fitted with 30 tonne bollard pull towing winch (1992) to provide alternative employment for her.

The Director of Marine Services (Naval) is also responsible for the contract management of the RAF and Army Range Safety Groups. The operation of both these organisations was offered for tender, with James Fisher & Sons being the successful tenderer. The contracts normally run for three years when they are again offered for competitive tender.

Details of Army Range Safety Craft are as follows:

Ship	Pennant Number	Completion Date	Builder
FALCONET	Y01	1983	James & Stone
PETARD	Y02	1983	James & Stone

G.R.T. 70 tons **Dimensions** 24m x 5.5m x 2.5m **Speed** 21 knots **Complement** 5.

There are also eleven smaller range safety craft; details below:

G.R.T. 19.68 tonnes **Dimensions** 14.9m x 4.66m x 1.67. **Speed** 22 knots **Complement** 3.

Their primary tasks are range surveillance and clearance, target towing for weapon attacks and the recovery of Sonabuoys, maritime weapons and training devices in coastal range areas. The craft are based at Pembroke Dock, Weymouth, Dover, Whitehaven and Loch Boisdale.

Details of RAF Range Craft are as follows:

LRRSC (Long Range Recovery and Support Craft)

Ship	Pennant Number	Completion Date	Builder
SEAL	5000	1967	Brooke Marine
SEAGULL	5001	1970	Fairmile Const.

G.R.T. 159 tons **Dimensions** 120' 3" x 23' 6" x 5' 11" **Speed** 21 knots **Complement** 6.

RTTL (Rescue, Target Towing Launches)

SPITFIRE, HALIFAX, HAMPDEN, HURRICANE, LANCASTER & WELLINGTON

G.R.T. 71 tons **Dimensions** 22m x 5.6m x 1.6m **Speed** 21 knots

There are also 3 x 63' Pinnaces Nos 1374, 1389 & 1392.

These craft are employed on target towing, SAR, various trials and weapon recovery. They are based at Invergordon, Great Yarmouth and Holyhead.

HMAV Ardennes

ARMY LANDING CRAFT
LCL CLASS (LANDING CRAFT LOGISTIC)

Vessel	Pennant Number	Completion Date	Builder
HMAV Ardennes	L4001	1977	Brooke Marine
HMAV Arakan	L4003	1978	Brooke Marine

Displacement 1,050 tons **Dimensions** 72m x 15m x 2m **Speed** 10 knots **Complement** 36.

Notes
Designed to carry up to 520 tonnes of cargo, overside loaded, or up to Five Chieftain tanks – Ro Ro loaded, reducing to 254 tonnes for beaching operations, through bow doors. Principal roles are maintenance of the Royal Artillery Range Outer Hebrides and in support of Amphibious Operations and Exercises.

95

ARMY VESSELS

● M. LENNON

RCTV Abbeville

RCL CLASS
(RAMPED CRAFT LOGISTIC)

Vessel	Pennant Number	Completion Date	Builder
RCTV Arromanches	L105	1981	Brooke Marine
RCTV Antwerp	L106	1981	Brooke Marine
RCTV Andalsnes	L107	1984	James & Stone
RCTV Abbeville	L108	1984	James & Stone
RCTV Akyab	L109	1984	James & Stone
RCTV Aachen	L110	1986	James & Stone
RCTV Arezzo	L111	1986	James & Stone
RCTV Agheila	L112	1987	James & Stone
RCTV Audemer	L113	1987	James & Stone

Displacement 165 tons **Dimensions** 33m x 8m x 1.5m **Speed** 9 knots **Complement** 6.

Notes
Smaller – "all purpose" landing craft capable of carrying up to 100 tons. In service in coastal waters around Cyprus, Hong Kong & UK.

Abinger

SEA CADET VESSELS

FLEET TENDERS 63 DESIGN

Ship	Pennant Number	Ship	Pennant Number
ABERDOVEY	Y10	ALNMOUTH	Y13
ABINGER	Y11	APPLEBY	A383

Displacement 117 tons **Dimensions** 24m x 5m x 3m **Speed** 10.5 knots.

Notes
'A' craft are allocated to the Sea Cadet Corps. ABERDOVEY, Southern Area, Portsmouth based; ABINGER, Eastern Area, Grimsby based; ALNMOUTH, North West Area, Liverpool based; APPLEBY, South West Area, based at Portland (summer) and Bristol (winter).
MEAVEY (A254) presently carries the name SULTAN VENTURER and operates from PORTSMOUTH for HMS SULTAN. Ex-BIBURY (A103) operates for Portsmouth Naval Base Sub Aqua Club.
MOD(N) also own and maintain ex IMS PAGHAM for the S.C.C based at Stranraer.

British Aerospace Sea Harrier

Variants: FRS 1 (FRS 2 undergoing development).
Role: Short take off, vertical landing (STOVL) fighter, reconnaissence and strike aircraft.
Engine: 1 x 21,500lb thrust Rolls Royce PEGASUS 104, 106 turbojet.
Span 25' 3" **length** 47' 7" **height** 12' 0" **Max weight** 26,200lb.
Max speed Mach 1.2 **Crew** 1 pilot.
Avionics: Blue Fox pulse radar. (To be replaced by the Blue Vixen pulse doppler radar in the FRS 2).
Armament: SEA EAGLE air to surface missiles. SIDEWINDER air to air missiles. (FRS 2 to carry the new Anglo/US AMRAAM radar guided air to air missiles). 2 x 30mm Aden cannons with 120 rounds per gun in detachable pods, one either side of the lower fuselage. 1 fuselage centreline and 4 underwing hardpoints. The inner wing stations are capable of carrying 2,000lb of stores and are plumbed for drop tanks. The other positions can carry stores up to 1,000lb in weight. Possible loads include 1,000lb, 500lb or practice bombs; BL 755 cluster bombs, Lepus flares, 190 or 100 gallon drop tanks. A single F95 camera is mounted obliquely in the nose for the reconnaissance role. The prototype FRS 2 first flew in September 1988 and sea trials took place in October 1990.
Squadron Service: 800, 801 and 899 squadrons in commission.
Notes: During 1993, 800 squadron will be embarked in HMS INVINCIBLE and 801 in HMS ARK ROYAL. 899 squadron is responsible for the training of replacement pilots and the development of tactics and is normally shore based at RNAS YEOVILTON. In a period of tension it could embark to reinforce the embarked air groups in the carriers.

● MARITIME PHOTOGRAPHIC

Westland SEA KING

Developed for the Royal Navy from the Sikorsky SH3D, the basic Sea King airframe is used in three different roles. The following details are common to all:
Engines: 2 x 1600shp Rolls Royce Gnome H 1400 – 1 free power turbines.
Rotor Diameter 62' 0" **Length** 54' 9" **Height** 17' 2" **Max Weight** 21,400lb **Max Speed** 125 knots.
The 3 versions are:-

● MARITIME PHOTOGRAPHIC

HAR 5 : HAS 6

The HAS6 has improved sonics, deeper dipping active sonar and Racal "Orange Crop 2" ESM
Roles: Anti-submarine search and strike. SAR. Transport.
Crew: 2 pilots, 1 observer and 1 aircrewman.
Avionics: MEL Sea Searcher radar; Plessey Type 195 variable depth active/passive sonar. GEC LAPADS passive sonobuoy analyses. Marconi Orange Crop passive ESM equipment.
Armament: 4 fuselage hardpoints capable of carrying STINGRAY torpedoes or depth charges. Various flares, markers, grenades and sonobuoys can be carried internally and hand launched. A 7.62mm machine gun can be mounted in the doorway.
Squadron Service: 771 Squadron operates the HAR 5, 810, 706, 814, 819, 820 and 826 squadrons in commission equipped with HAS 6.
Notes: The Sea King has been the backbone of the Fleet Air Arm's anti-submarine force since 1970. 706 is the advanced training squadron at RNAS CULDROSE. 810 is an operational training squadron with the capability to embark to reinforce the front line. During 1993, 814 squadron will be embarked in HMS INVINCIBLE and 820 in HMS ARK ROYAL. 819 is shore based at PRESTWICK and 826 provides Flights deployed in frigates and RFAs. The HAR 5 operates with a noteable SAR capability which is frequently demonstrated in the south west approaches. The HAS 6 has less complete SAR facilities

AEW 2

Role: Airborne Early Warning. **Crew:** 1 pilot and 2 observers.
Avionics: Thorn/EMI Searchwater radar. Marconi Orange Crop passive ESM equipment.
Armament: Nil.
Squadron Service: 849 HQ, 849A and 849B flights in commission.
Notes: Used to detect low flying aircraft trying to attack aircraft carrier battle groups under shipborne radar cover. Can also be used for surface search utilising its sophisticated, computerised long range radar. During 1993 849A flight will be embarked in HMS INVINCIBLE and 849B in HMS ARK ROYAL. 849HQ acts as a training and trials unit at RNAS CULDROSE.

HC 4

Role: Commando assault and utility transport.
Crew: 1 pilot and 1 aircrewman.
Armament: Door mounted 7.62mm machine gun.
Squadron Service: 707, 772, 845 and 846 squadrons in commission.
Notes: Capable of carrying up to 27 troops in the cabin or a wide variety of underslung loads up to 8,000lb in weight. 707 squadron is a training unit at RNAS YEOVILTON. 845 and 846 squadrons are based at YEOVILTON but able to embark or detach at short notice to support 3 Commando Brigade. The Sea King HC4 has a fixed undercarriage with no sponsons and no radome.

● OFFICIAL PHOTO

Westland LYNX

Variants: HAS 3, HAS 3S, HAS 3CTS.
Roles: Surface search and strike; anti-submarine strike; SAR.
Engines: 2 x 900hp Rolls Royce GEM BS 360-07-26 free shaft turbines.
Rotor diameter: 42'0" **Length** 39' 1¹/4" **Height** 11',0" **Max Weight** 9,500lb.
Max Speed: 150 knots. **Crew:** 1 pilot and 1 observer.
Avionics: Ferranti SEA SPRAY radar. Racal Orange Crop passive ESM equipment.
Armament: External pylons carry up to 4 x SEA SKUA air to surface missiles or 2 x STINGRAY, Mk 46 torpedoes, depth charges, flares or markers.
Squadron Service: 702, 815 (815 OEU FLT) and 829 squadrons in commission.
Notes: 815 OEU FLT is a trials squadron with equipment for HAS 8 and 702 is a training squadron based at RNAS PORTLAND. 815, also based at Portland is the parent unit for single aircraft flights that embark in Type 42 destroyers and some classes of frigate, specialising in the surface strike role. 829 squadron parents flights in the Type 22 and other anti-submarine frigates. A version of the Lynx, the AH1, is operated by the Royal Marines Brigade Air Squadron which is based at RNAS Yeovilton.
(HAS Mk 8) is now flying and undergoing intensive development trials.
HAS 3S represents the first phase of developments that will lead to the HAS 8; the HAS 3CTS represents the second phase and full HAS 8 aircraft are expected to be delivered in the mid 90's.

Westland GAZELLE HT2

Engine: 1 x 592shp Turbomeca ASTAZOU free power turbine.
Crew: 1 or 2 pilots.
Notes: In service with 705 squadron at RNAS CULDROSE. Used for training all RN helicopter pilots up to "wings standard" before they move onto the Sea King or Lynx. A version of the Gazelle, the AH1, is used by the Royal Marines Brigade Air Squadron based at RNAS Yeovilton.

OTHER AIRCRAFT TYPES IN ROYAL NAVY SERVICE DURING 1993

British Aerospace JETSTREAM T2 and T3

Engines: 2 x 940hp Turbomeca ASTAZOU 16D turboprops. (T3 Garrett turboprops).
Crew: 1 or 2 pilots, 2 student observers plus 3 other seats.
Notes: A number of these aircraft are used by 750 squadron at RNAS CULDROSE for training Fleet Air Arm Observers and also by the Heron flight at RNAS Yeovilton.

de Havilland CHIPMUNK

Engine: 1 x 145hp de Havilland Gipsy Major 8 piston engine.
Crew: 2 pilots.
Notes: Used by the RN Flying Grading Flight at Roborough airport near Plymouth (and as such the first aircraft flown by generations of naval aircrew) and by stations flights at RNAS CULDROSE and YEOVILTON.

British Aerospace CANBERRA TT18

Engines: 2 x 6500lb thrust Rolls Royce AVON turbojets.
Crew: 1 pilot and 1 observer.
Notes: Used by the (civilian manned) Fleet Requirements and Aircraft Direction Unit (FRADU) at RNAS YEOVILTON. Canberras provide towed targets for live firings by ships at sea. Only 2 remain in service to be replaced by Falcon aircraft on contract to MOD(N).

Hawker HUNTER T8, GA11, T7 & T8M

Engine: 1 x 7575lb thrust Rolls Royce AVON turbojet.
Crew: T8 1 or 2 pilots. GA11 1 pilot. T7 1 or 2 pilots. T8m 1 or 2 pilots.
Notes: The Royal Navy has used Hunters to train fixed wing pilots since 1958. A number remain in service at RNAS YEOVILTON with the RN flying standards flight and with FRADU who use them as airborne targets for the aircraft direction school. 899 Squadron also use these aircraft as radar trainers for Sea Harrier pilots.

In addition to these aircraft, the following aircraft have naval functions:
CANBERRA T17: Used by 360 joint RN/RAF Squadron for electronic warfare tasks. Based at RAF WYTON.
British Aerospace 125: Two aircraft, owned by the RN are operated by RN aircrew as part of 32 Squadron RAF based at RAF NORTHOLT.
The Fleet Air Arm Historic flight based at RNAS YEOVILTON has a **SWORDFISH, SEAHAWK, FIREFLY and TIGER MOTH** on strength and these are often seen at air displays in the summer months. The future of the Seahawk is in doubt.

Full details of these and many other naval aircraft can be found in the revised edition of AIRCRAFT OF THE ROYAL NAVY SINCE 1945 published by Maritime Books.

At the end of the line ...

Readers may well find other warships afloat which are not mentioned in this book. The majority have fulfilled a long and useful life and are now relegated to non-seagoing duties. The following list gives details of their current duties:

Pennant Number	Ship	Remarks
A134	RAME HEAD	Escort Maintenance Vessel – now Royal Marines Training Ship at Portland
C35	BELFAST	World War II Cruiser Museum ship – Pool of London (Open to the public) Tel: 071-407 6434
D73	CAVALIER	World War II Destroyer Museum Ship at Hebburn Not open to public. Future under consideration.
D12	KENT	County Class Destroyer – Sea Cadet Training Ship at Portsmouth. Future "under consideration"
F126	PLYMOUTH	Type 12 Frigate & Oberon class submarine Museum Ships at Birkenhead
S21	ONYX	Open to the public daily. Tel: 051 650 1573
S11	ORPHEUS	Oberon Class Submarine Harbour Training Ship at Gosport
S67	ALLIANCE	Submarine – Museum Ship at Gosport Open to the public. Tel: 0705 - 511485

At the time of publishing the following ships were awaiting tow for scrap or sale.

PORTSMOUTH		ROSYTH	PLYMOUTH
Charybdis	Jupiter	Churchill	Conqueror
Cleopatra	Minerva	Dreadnought	Courageous
Hecate	Juno	Revenge	Warspite
Hermione	Sentinel	Swiftsure	Regent